D1634700

BRITISH SAMPLERS

A Concise History

BRITISH SAMPLERS

A Concise History

by

JANE TOLLER

CULTURAL EXHIBITIONS

with

PHILLIMORE

1980

Published by
PHILLIMORE & CO. LTD.
Shopwyke Hall, Chichester, Sussex, England
in association with
CULTURAL EXHIBITIONS LTD.
8 Meadrow, Godalming, Surrey, England

ISBN 0 85033 383 0

Printed in Great Britain by
GRAPHIC COLOUR PRINT
Emsworth, Hants.

CONTENTS

LIST OF ILLUSTRATIONS

Front Cover: *Illustration of work done by the Bird family at Hopton school, 1789; coloured silks on tammy* (photo: Mr. Frith, of Messrs. Hills and Saunders, Eton)

FOREWORD

Jane Toller is a highly respected and well-known dealer in antiques, and author of a number of books about them. Her knowledge is based on a lifetime experience in her chosen career.

Only a few books on samplers have been published recently and now this one has been added, inspired by her special interest in them.

Many people nowadays are fascinated by and attracted to these charming souvenirs of a bygone and more leisured age. This interest has resulted in an increasing difficulty in finding them by the aspiring and also established collector, and in the greatly augmented prices they are fetching, especially at auction.

Her knowledge is far from being only academic, for she has an extensive experience of their conservation and all that this entails. In this connection she has written a valuable and helpful chapter on their care.

In successive chapters she takes the reader from the reason for samplers, through the different centuries, with their special characteristics, and ends with a description of those from Scotland, Ireland, Wales, and America. In the latter chapter she alludes to one of the best collections in that country belonging to Theodore H. Kapnek, a personal friend of hers.

The few illustrations, all that are needed, are excellent.

This book is intended to be a short account of the subject and one which can be easily carried around for reference. It will be instructive and of interest not only to the would-be collector, but to the specialist as well.

D. GOODHART

ACKNOWLEDGEMENTS

I am greatly indebted to the following for their enthusiastic co-operation and help with this book.

Dr. D. Goodhart, Mr. Theodore H. Kapnek, U.S.A., Mr. and Mrs. Scaramanga, Mrs. Webster Speekeman, Mrs. Laven Jones of the Ulster Folk Museum, Mrs. I. E. Anthony of St. Fagans Museum, Cardiff and the librarians of the Eton branch of the Berkshire County Council.

Chapter 1

THE REASON FOR SAMPLERS

EVERYONE who becomes interested in samplers invariably asks the same question: 'When were they started in England, and why?'

There is reason to believe that a few existed in the 15th century, and good evidence to know that they were being made in the 16th. The account book for Elizabeth of York in 1502 contains this entry:

> 'To Thomas Fische for an elle of lynnyn cloth
> for a sampler for the Queen'

In the will of Margaret Thomas, dated 1546, she leaves her

> 'sampler with semes to Alys Pinchbeck'

and Shakespeare, in '*A Midsummer Night's Dream*', has

> 'We Hermia, like two artificial girls
> Have with our needles created one flower
> Both on one sampler, sitting on one cushion.'

But to understand the reason for samplers, it is as well to know something of the history of English ecclesiastical needlework, which up to the end of the 15th century had been famous all over Europe.

This was the work of nuns (and even in some cases of monks) that occupied the great religious houses of Britain. The embroidery wrought by them enriched such vestments as copes, albs, dalmatics, chasubles, stoles, mitres, and so on, and also altar frontals, dossals, curtains, and banners. Those were made of velvets, silks, satins and brocades embroidered with coloured silks and gold and silver threads, and enriched by the use of precious stones and pearls.

There was much embroidery, too, on the plain white vestments and altar linen. Many famous pieces of this ecclesiastical embroidery have miraculously survived, and are beautifully displayed at the Victoria and Albert Museum, London.

In the 16th century two fatal blows were struck at this craft: (1) The Reformation, when all such vestments and hangings were ordered to be moved from every place of worship; and (2) The Dissolution of the religious houses under Henry VIII, when both monks and nuns were disbanded. Some of them fled abroad, taking their treasured vestments with them. The Syon Cope—more famous perhaps than any other—was taken abroad by the Brigidine nuns from the Syon Convent at Isleworth, Middlesex, when they were forced to leave England to seek shelter elsewhere. After centuries of travelling from nunnery to nunnery, it came back with the Order when it returned to England from Lisbon in 1820. Finally, it became the property of the nation.

But not much escaped so miraculously. A great deal was pulled to pieces in order to secure the valuable gold and silver threads. Other pieces were annexed by the spoilers to adorn their own houses. Naturally, anything used in this way has not lasted. Vestments and hangings which had been kept with loving care in religious houses, abbeys and cathedrals could not stand up to the constant wear of ordinary household use. So gradually most of our fine ecclesiastical embroidery disappeared, and not only were the fabrics lost, but unhappily the designs that had been used for this embroidery could be seen no longer. There were now no nuns being trained to teach these designs to others, and this source of fresh designs was now lost forever.

The daughters of the upper classes had often been sent to nunneries to be educated, and needlework was a necessary accomplishment which all girls had to learn. The subject included embroidery to decorate the garments of both men and women, and also the household linen. Girls now had to be taught needlework at home, either by their mothers or by the 'sewing-women' who were employed specially to help with all this work. (One wonders whether Catholic households employed some of the destitute nuns in this capacity.) By the end of the 16th century it was not only the upper classes that needed sewing-women. The new middle class of rich merchants and opulent craftsmen from the city guilds had grown enormously. They had built comfortable houses for themselves with the larger windows which were now becoming fashionable. The curtains for these, judging by contemporary paintings of interiors, were of plain coloured cloth or velvet decorated with wide bands of embroidery. Beds also had to be furnished with embroidered hangings, and there were table-cloths and cushion covers to be wrought. So embroidery, for-bidden for ecclesiastic uses, was coming far more into fashion, not only for household furnishings, but for the clothing of both sexes. By the end of the 16th century hardly any piece of outer clothing seems to have been made without the use of embroidery —it even extended to gloves, scarves, bonnets and hats—and Elizabethan dress would have been considered dowdy without it. No wonder quite small children had to start learning it, and sewing-women became necessities for the staffing of quite modest households.

Where were the designs for this varied needlework to be found? There were printed books of designs in Germany at this time, but they did not appear in England until much later and were then too expensive for an average household to buy. Instead, every needlewoman made her own pattern book, incorporating stitches she remembered from childhood, or those collected from friends.

Without doubt, many ideas for designs were taken from ancient stone or wood carvings, or from books illustrating birds, flowers, or beasts. These were all worked on to a strip of rather coarse unbleached linen not more than eight or nine inches wide. The embroideress stitched her ideas on to fabric instead of drawing them on paper. The result of all this highly specialized work was then called an 'ensampler', or more simply, a 'sampler'. It could be used as a reference whenever or where-ever embroidery was needed. When not in use, it was rolled up and kept in a drawer or sewing-box.

These early samplers were never intended to be used as pictures, and indeed, any that survived were not treated as such until the beginning of the 20th century, when antique furniture became fashionable and family samplers—usually 18th and 19th century work—were hung on walls. The very early samplers, however, were not popular. They contained no pictures and the colours were not bright enough. In cases where they *were* framed, it seems to have been done by amateurs using any old frame that might be obtainable. Many valuable samplers have been found stuffed into frames too small for them, which has resulted in ends being turned in or edges cut to make them fit. No trouble was taken to see that they were really dustproof; they were the Cinderellas of the sampler fashion. Their owners would be astonished indeed to find how much these 'ugly old samplers' are now valued, eagerly sought after, and treasured when found. As far as these early samplers are concerned, the Cinderella story has come true.

1. Early Sampler of Designs. Worked in coloured silks on linen. Faint tracing lines of a motif can be seen in the bottom left-hand corner. Dated 1640 (*C. & J. Toller*)

14

Chapter 2

17th-CENTURY SAMPLERS

THERE ARE SEVERAL 17th-century samplers to be found at the present day. I have had at least half-a-dozen through my own hands, and known of several others in private collections. The Victoria and Albert Museum has several, as have other museums throughout Great Britain.

Those I have seen are in remarkably good condition, due, I believe, to the fact that they were all worked on linen, which is a hard-wearing material and not liable to the damage done by the ravages of time, moths, and so on. Quite a few of these early samplers were brought to public notice in 1977, when one or two collections were offered for sale by the leading London sale-rooms, and aroused great interest in the Press because of the high prices they fetched at auction.

Early samplers can be divided into sections, as follows:

Section 1

Those which contain scattered motifs worked in coloured silks on backgrounds of coarse unbleached linen (see Plate 1). The motifs are stylized flowers, such as Tudor roses and other similar emblems, carnations, honeysuckle, tulips, crocus, and strawberries; geometric designs made in shapes that would easily join on to each other; and exotic creatures such as lizards, butterflies, caterpillars and other insects. This last class were copied from illustrations in books on the subject published at this time. Small creatures naturally had to be *enlarged* for these illustrations; therefore, a page of butterflies and caterpillars would be of much the same dimensions as the lions and unicorns on the next page. The embroideress would naturally trace these designs straight from the illustrations on

15

to her needlework. Consequently, we get the delightfully non-sensical pictures in samplers and the fashionable 'stump-work' of the period, of kings and queens walking quite unalarmed among moths as large as stags, and birds much bigger than the trees they perch upon; or, as I saw recently in one sampler, a swarm of bees as big as the flight of birds above them!

Section 2

In this class the style of the sampler changed and became more formal. The various motifs were gathered into definite patterns instead of being scattered haphazardly on the canvas. The sampler was of white or cream linen embroidered with coloured silks: pale greens, blues, pinks and yellows, and gold and silver threads were now being used. The idea was to fill the sampler with bands of varying embroidery about two or three inches wide. Each band was divided from the next by a very narrow differing band of embroidery. A clever idea for making a pattern was to fill up each bar with rows of the same emblem (Tudor roses was the favourite) that could be fitted in alternatively *upside down*, whatever the motif used. This method always seems to have been adopted, and as designs look quite different upside down, the embroiderers did not tire of repeating it, especially if the colours were changed. It certainly looks very well, and shows a great deal of trouble was taken.

Section 3

An indication that children were being set to work on samplers is given by the fact that alphabets and numerals were included. The name of the child, her age, and probably the date of completion was embroidered wherever there happened to be room for it; it was of secondary importance to the embroidery. In order that she should absorb a little moral or scriptural learning while employed on her needlework, a text, usually from the Book of Proverbs in the Old Testament, was generally included. The alphabet at this time was worked in Gothic (pointed) scripts, and this practice continued until about 1720 (which was curious, for Italic handwriting had by then been in normal usage for some time). This Gothic lettering is often a stumbling block to the sampler 'reader', because some of the letters are different from those we use today. For instance, the letter 'A' often had the bar across the top, instead of the middle, thus **Π**. There was no 'J' at all, the reason being that at this time the letter 'I' was used for a 'J', usually with a small bar across the middle, thus I. 'U' was represented quite often by the 'V', and the letter double 'V' was therefore given as 'W'.

The child, often as young as six years old, obviously could not understand what she was copying so painstakingly, for frequently we find no stops or commas, and capital letters used quite haphazardly. And to make matters more confusing for the modern collector, a word was often started with the first two letters at the end of a line and the rest of the word followed on the next line, with little or no space between each word.

Here is an example, worked by a child of six. The letters were Gothic capitals, very intricate in design and beautifully embroidered:

'THISWORKWASWR
OUGHTBY'

and then her name followed. This practice was made more difficult by the fact that no punctuation marks were used, so that deciphering a not very well-known scriptural text becomes quite a problem.

Rows of numerals in different forms of writing followed the alphabet. This exercise was necessary. Linen, both personal and household, had to be marked, and in those days marking ink had not been invented. Everything had to be marked by hand, not only with the name, but the date when it was finished.

This form of sampler continued well into the first quarter of the 18th century, with one interesting difference: as well as unbleached or white linen, *coloured* backgrounds of pink or yellow became popular. Gold and silver thread was most effective when used on these colours.

Section 4

The samplers in this class are of a different type altogether from the preceding ones, the only similarity being in the shape and style, i.e., they were long and narrow, and worked in 'bars'.

These exquisite pieces of needlework were done in 'cut'- or 'drawn'-work, which had the appearance of lace, and lace had been much in fashion during the last two centuries for both male and female costumes. These cut-work samplers are often referred to as 'lace samplers', which conveys a wrong impression to the new collector, who imagines them to be either of pillow-lace or lace worked on net. They are neither. 'Cut-work' means filling in an open space (cut purposely) with thread stretched across, and across again diagonally at one-inch intervals, and then button-holed into various patterns (see Plate 19). It must have been a very interesting occupation. I have mended several torn or missing pieces in this cut-work, and found it most engrossing. This work was usually done on a white linen ground with white thread. Each 'bar' of cut-work varied from the next. By way of contrast, bars of plain needle-work in geometrical designs were worked between each cut-work pattern. I believe that this was the kind of needlework wherein metal threads could certainly *not* be used. 'Drawn-thread' work has a certain similarity in appearance, but the linen is not cut; instead, various threads are removed from the linen, and the desired pattern then formed by drawing the remaining threads together into different designs with needle and thread.

Stitches used in 17th-century samplers

Buttonhole; braid; chain; cross and half-cross; double running; eyelet holes; hemstitch; Hungarian point; Italian cross; long-stemmed cross; knotted; ladder; oriental; overlapping herring-bone; rococo; satin; tent. On the 'lace' or cut-work samplers, needlepoint, lace fillings, drawn-thread work, darning and French knots were also used.

2. A very beautiful sampler which, judging by the costumes and general outlay must be very early 18th century. The alphabet and motifs are worked between different patterned edges. Underneath is a picture of a shepherd and shepherdess under trees with sheep, a dalmatian dog and butterflies, and insects which seem to have strayed in from some Stump Work. Silk on fine canvas.

Chapter 3

18th-CENTURY SAMPLERS

OUR HISTORY of 18th-century samplers takes us for 20 years into that of the 19th. It must be remembered, however, that we did not enter it until 1720. One cannot pin dates down when referring to anything antique. For instance, Queen Anne furniture did not come to a stop immediately upon her death, but was carried through into the reign of George I.

It was during the years 1720-1820 that samplers for the collector reached their peak of interest, not only in Great Britain, but in America also. This period, as far as stitchery is concerned, is usually referred to as the 18th century.

In about 1720 the style and shape of the sampler changed almost entirely. It was no longer a 'sampler' of stitches, but a form of education for girls in the age group of 8-15 years, and a 'leaving task' for the young ladies at finishing schools and academies.

People nowadays often pity these children, who it seems had to spend long hours doing such fine needlework when they might have been doing something more beneficial for their health and happiness. But it was only for a certain portion of the day that this task was done, and if they had any gift for fine sewing and embroidery they possibly enjoyed it hugely, for there was a great deal to amuse a child in a sampler of this period.

The canvas used for the purpose had changed from linen to a woollen cloth called 'tammy', made specially for embroidery because it was much easier to work on than linen. It was, I have always considered, an unfortunate change, but then the manufacturers could not have foreseen the difficulties that would arise in the future by its use. Wool is prone to moth, and also to the staining caused through dark wood backings, and many

3. An outstandingly fine sampler giving examples of topiary. Two separate flower borders, the inner of free embroidery, the outer of stereotyped flowers. Two flying angels are blowing trumpets, and swinging censers, on either side of a large crown. Dated 1766.

4.   A very interesting sampler combining early motifs with 'lace' work. The alphabet all enclosed in a lace border. Worked in silks on linen. Dated 1767.

fine samplers have been irretrievably ruined through its use. Enthusiastic owners at different times, perhaps not realizing the wool content, have washed these tammy samplers in soap and water. Wool shrinks, but silk used for embroidery thread does not, and no amount of pressing will ever completely flatten the 'bobbly' appearance of bunched wool between the motifs and designs that go to the making of samplers.

There was now a wider choice of colours which were freely and enthusiastically used, and in order to get as much into the sampler as possible, the size became much wider and as long as was deemed necessary. Samplers were now being used more and more for pictures as the century moved on, so they were no longer hemmed or hemstitched, but tacked down to the rim of a wooden stretcher when finished.

The layout of the 18th-century sampler was as follows: several types of alphabet and numerals; a verse or text, and then the main picture—whatever that might be—surrounded by every kind of motif. Very often among these were the initials of each member of both sides of the family—paternal on the left, maternal on the right—and worked in black if deceased. The child's name and age were included, usually at the beginning or end. Very often the date of completion was added. A narrow border, usually of flowers or a geometric design, ran all round the edge of the sampler. The background was not covered by a 'filling-in stitch', as the contemporary needlework pictures were, but was practically covered with every kind of motif. The designs for these had obviously been taken from earlier samplers. As for the alphabets, Italic script was now used, and two forms were given: capitals and small letters. In both cases the letter 'J' appeared, and also 'U' and 'W'. Instead of a text, verses were used, generally those of a well-known hymn or verses of a highly filial nature, extolling their parents, and thanking them for the way they had educated their child. The main picture came next. The prime favourite was Adam and Eve on either side of the apple tree, round which the serpent was coiled. Eve was holding an apple, and occasionally Adam was too. Their costumes, or lack of them, were highly diverting. Other favourites included a ship in full sail; a shepherdess and her sheep; male and female figures wearing the fashionable clothes of the

5. 'Alphabets and Numerals'. Coloured silks on linen. A fine example of different alphabets and figures used in the marking of linen. Worked by Elizabeth Clark, 1826. (*C. & J. Toller*)

period; soldiers and sailors; and, of course, that great feature of all children's art, the house in which they lived. Castles, mansions, country houses, modest Georgian dwellings with steps leading up to the front door, lots of windows, a steeply-pitched roof and tall chimneys; all were depicted. Some were even supplied with stables, dovecotes and dog kennels!

Other space-fillers were flying angels, lions, unicorns, stags, horses, cats, squirrels, rabbits, caterpillars, bees and butterflies, and a great multiplicity of birds, none of which was ever to scale.

Crowns appeared in profusion (and not only in connection with the Royal Arms). They frequently occurred over the initials (previously mentioned) and one wonders whether this was an indication that the owner was titled. Household objects such as tables and chairs, cradles, lanterns, candlesticks and pottery were charmingly depicted. The social history all these items convey and the unconscious humour that was portrayed in them has made these 18th-century samplers highly popular.

Parents would seem to have been very proud of their children's work, for whether they were done under tuition at home or as school-leaving tasks, they were framed and hung up for the admiration of relations and friends.

The frames varied. Some were of broad gilded wood, often with black glass and gilt mounts. Some were in the more sombre narrow black 'Hogarth' frames, and those of a later period had narrow frames of rosewood or mahogany. (Bird's-eye maple was not used until later in the 19th century, when it became a fashionable wood for framing almost every type of picture.)

An expert needlewoman, examining the actual stitches used in these 18th-century samplers will find that the popular idea that they were worked entirely in cross (or tent) stitch is quite wrong. There are at least nine different types of cross-stitch, for instance. Other stitches used included rococo, Hungarian cross, oriental, buttonhole, chain, double-running, knotted, stem, satin and eyelet. A different kind of stitch was used for border and band work, besides the numerous ones used in cut-work (a 17th-century fashion often introduced into 18th-century samplers). Actually, much trouble must have been taken to decide what combination of stitch would suit each motif best. These motifs,

6. 'Flowers and Insects'. This is worked on very fine linen with coloured silks, and has a charmingly irregular border of flowers. The text is 'Sarah Burket. Working in the 9th year of her age 1797'.

it must be remembered, were used to fill in the background around the text or main subject. British samplers were rarely filled in with cross-stitch. In many cases the main subject, verses, name and age, surrounded by an embroidered border, were considered all that was necessary. The rest of the canvas, whether of linen, tammy or gauze, was left uncovered.

The designs for samplers of this period were first drawn on the canvas (as they had been on earlier linen curtains or bed-spreads). I have noticed traces of grey or pale blue lines on unfinished samplers, and on a length of linen with 17th-century silk embroidery I found the design pencilled in terra-cotta.

Later on, I have no doubt that designs were *traced* from illustrations in books. I give an old recipe for tracing paper below:

Black paper for drawing patterns

Mix and smooth lamp-black and sweet oil with a bit of flennel, cover a sheet or two of large writing paper with this mixture; then dab the paper dry with a bit of fine linen and keep it by for using in the following manner:

Put the black side on another sheet of paper and fasten with a small pin. Lay on the back of the black paper the pattern to be drawn, and go over it with the point of a steel pencil: the black paper will then leave the impression of the pattern on the under sheet, on which you must now draw it with ink.

If you draw patterns on cloth or muslin, do it with a pen dipped in a bit of stone blue, a bit of sugar and a little water, mixed smooth in a teacup, in which it will be always ready for use; if fresh, wet to a due consistence as wanted.

Darning Samplers

The 17th-century cut-work and drawn-thread work was now replaced by these samplers, which made their appearance in about 1780, when extra fine needles were being made. These darning samplers were worked on fine linen or gauze. At least six different methods of darning were used, each occupying about three square inches, filling the sides and one end of the sampler (the middle space being filled by a bunch of flowers in ordinary embroidery). The space at the bottom contained the name, date of completion and age of the child. When the darning examples occupied the *middle* of the canvas, a wreath of naturalistic flowers was embroidered all round them. The darns were done in different coloured fine silk thread. This is the type of work that should be framed between *two pieces of glass*, in order to exhibit the extreme fineness of the work, which is as well done on the back as on the front in an almost unbelievable manner (see Plate 7).

It has been supposed that a hole (about one inch square) was first cut in the material which had to be darned. I say 'supposed' because on close examination of those I have removed from their frames for cleaning purposes, I have discovered that in fact these holes were *not* cut. The middle of the darn was done 'in the air' *above* the material which, in a way, makes it a much more difficult feat.

27

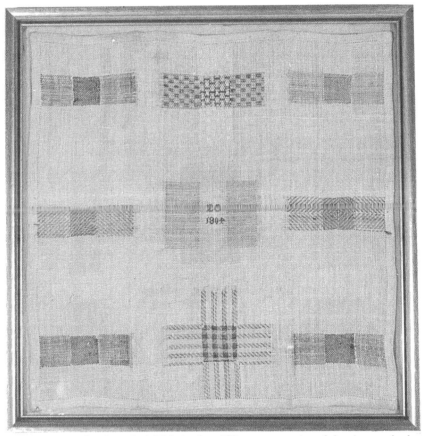

7. 'A Darning Sampler'. This is nine different examples of darning worked on a superfine linen hemstitched square in different coloured silks. The sample itself is only 11 ins. x 11 ins. so each darn can only be about 3½ ins. A remarkable feat of needlework. *c.*1790.

It is a rather curious fact that, though I have seen many beautifully neat darns on ancient garments, sheets, curtains, and so on, the ordinary darning stitch has always been used, and not one of the examples worked on a 'darning' sampler. Perhaps the work was just done as an exercise in superfine needlework and not for utilitarian purposes.

These darning samplers are rare, and perhaps not very exciting at a casual glance, as they are not highly coloured; but they are intensely interesting to needlework experts, and no good collection should be without one.

A few verses from 18th-century samplers

> This I did to let you see,
> What care my parents took of me.

And from a charity school sampler:

> I did this work, I thank my God,
> Without correction of the rod.

> Had I the world at my command,
> The treasures of the sea and land,
> And should I all the world bestow,
> It would not pay the debt I owe.

Worked by Eliza Yates aged 9 at Sileby School Leicestershire

> Virtue is the chiefest beauty of the mind,
> The noblest ornament of womankind,
> Virtue is our safeguard and our guiding star,
> That stirs up reason when our senses err.
>
> Ann Watts aged 8 years

8. 'Queen's Palace' (Now Buckingham Palace). Worked in coloured silks on tammy. Worked by Margaret Snowden, *c.*1820. *(C. & J. Toller)*

9. Map of England. Worked on gauze mounted on linen in black and coloured threads in Tambour stitch. Early 19th century.   (*C. & J. Toller*)

Chapter 4

19th-CENTURY SAMPLERS AND MAPS

NEEDLEWORK MAPS came into fashion towards the end of the 18th century, but as the greater majority were worked in the early 19th century, I am including them in this chapter. Though not strictly samplers, I feel they should be classed with them, because they quite obviously took the place of samplers as a method of teaching certain kinds of embroidery (with a secondary subject of geography). They must have been done on a large frame, as most of them measure from about eighteen inches to two feet long. Many schools set them for a 'leaving task', and one often finds the name of the school where it was worked finely embroidered in black in a small cartouche somewhere on the top right-hand side, together with the name of the girl who worked it, and the date it was finished. The outline of the map was worked in a 'tambour' stitch, i.e., a species of chain stitch, for which a long continuous thread was needed. Instead of a needle, a very fine crochet hook was used. This was pushed vertically through the material to pick up the thread held there by the left hand of the embroideress (the thread running from a revolving skein holder). This is a quick method of making a chain stitch for it does not involve threading and rethreading a needle.

There are two distinct types of these maps:

A large rectangular shape with the outline of the map (usually of Great Britain) outlined in coloured silks on a background of tammy gauze or linen. The countries were outlined in fine black silk, and the names filled in, using either small capitals or Italian script. In each county, *where there was room, the main towns might be given.* England and Wales were fully furnished with counties, towns and rivers, but Scotland and Ireland were usually given only in part, with perhaps the names

31

10. A very charming combination of sampler and embroidery stitches worked in coloured silks on tammy, in a choice mahogany frame of the period (about 1800).

of one or two places and rivers. These maps were framed in black or gilt frames, the latter occasionally with a gilded black inset oval mount.

The other map of Great Britain was worked in coloured silks on a large oval of either satin or taffetas. Round the map ran an outer border of delicately coloured flowers. Usually embroidered in the top right-hand corner was the seated figure of Britannia, helmeted, with a trident in her hand, a shield or cornucopia on the ground by her side, and the British lion *couchant* at her feet. A man-o-war in full sail was somewhere in the background, the whole being worked in reds, whites and blues. These were framed in broad gilt oval frames.

In the 18th century there was a girls' finishing school at Marlow, in Buckinghamshire, in a house in St. Peter's Street (now known as *The Fisherman's Retreat*). These oval needle-work maps were a sort of trade mark of the school. Every family of importance in the district must have had a daughter there, because the maps quite often turned up at big house sales in the district during the middle of this century, when their owners began to find it was growing impossible to staff such large places. The maps found ready purchasers, for they are very decorative, but unfortunately the materials on which they were embroidered—thin silk or satin—are inclined to split, having very little ability to stand the strong light in which they had been hanging or had been placed by their new owners.

While on the subject of maps, I cannot forbear to tell the story of one I saw, and kept on seeing as it passed from hand to hand in the trade. It was fascinatingly amusing, and I strongly suspect that the girl who did it was not good at embroidery but still wished to be in the fashion. The map was not on canvas, but on a good paper background:

In the early 19th century it was possible to buy ready-made coloured chenille cords. The outlines of this map were 'couched' on with this cord, and the names of the places neatly inscribed in Indian ink instead of being worked in black silk thread. The map was in an imposing frame, and, until one took a really close look, could very well have passed as an *embroidered* map. But it deserves mention here as a clever piece of ingenuity. The Royal Scottish Museum in Edinburgh has a map of Ireland

The sampler text reads:

Jesus prmit thy Gracious name to stand ·
As the first labours of an infant hand!
And while my fingers on my sampler move,
Do thou instruct my mind to know thy love
Thy Spirits Graces to my soul impart ·
And write the name of Jesus on my heart ·

Margaret Strick's
Sampler
finished March 6 th 1834 Aged 14

11. 'Adam and Eve'. A typical sampler of the period depicting a wonderful crop of apples on the tree, a very lusty serpent and many other motifs. Worked with silk on linen. Worked by Margaret Strick in 1834.

34

worked in black thread on a white cotton background. In the top left-hand corner is a tree worked in coloured chenille thread, under which are the initials 'C.H.' and the date 1847. It is interesting to note that some forty years earlier chenille threads were much used in English needlework to depict grass, trees and foliage.

Besides maps of Britain, there were maps of other parts of Europe. I had a very interesting one of the Western Hemisphere beautifully worked on white satin with fine black silks. The pattern had already been outlined on the material by the makers, Laurie and Writtle, of 53 Fleet Street, London (dated 1797).

The most unusual map I ever had was a plan of the 'Pilgrim's Progress'. All the names of the places the pilgrim went through were named and illustrated in needlework on this map; probably it was unique, for I have never seen or heard of another.

As I have said, the 19th century started to differ from its predecessor around 1820–30. After that the pictorial sampler seemed to cease and its place as main feature was taken by lengthier wording: either the whole of the Lord's Prayer or the Ten Commandments; all the verses of one of Mr. Wesley's hymns, or three or four pious verses from some other poem. The words were usually done in fine black silk, but colour was introduced by a wide border of stylized flowers. These were fashionable until about 1840, by which time fashions had changed, in England that is. Embroidered flower pictures in cross-stitch or Berlin wool in very bright colours, or exotic birds in cut-wool work were now all the rage, to be closely followed by copies of famous paintings worked most meticulously in wool. Bead-work was used for foot stools, or small hanging 'face-screens'. Embroidered slippers, waistcoats, or smoking caps, with detailed instructions and diagrams, were given in all the ladies' magazines. Wool-work was in with a big bang, and samplers now quite a thing of the past. (But Wales, Scotland and Ireland continued with the sampler almost to the 1860's.) Their place was taken then by embroidered wool-work texts or verses, worked on a stout paper canvas, and framed in maple or painted wooden frames. The work was well done, but deadly dull, and intended mostly for the decoration of small cottage parlours or children's bedrooms. There are still some around and I suppose one ought to be included in a collection of any size.

These pictures must have led to the fashion of cross-stitch bookmarkers, worked on a piece of paper canvas about 6 ins x 2 ins. A text, or a birthday wish for a friend, was worked on this in coloured silks, and it was then stitched to a piece of ribbon the same colour as the silks, the same width and about twice the length of the canvas. They were used in large bound books of poems, or the family Bible, but were quickly supplemented by the Stevengraph woven silk bookmarkers.

The period of the sampler stretches over a period of about 350 years, from 1520 1870. Happily, many of these have been well preserved. A great many can be seen in museums. The later ones can still be bought. Many times when I have painstakingly been mending samplers I have looked at the date and imagined myself back in the time when they were worked—the Stuarts, Cromwellians and Queen Anne; Hanoverians, Jacobites; Trafalgar and Waterloo, even the Industrial Revolution—a different bit of history in each one, captured in needlework by some child blissfully unconscious of what was going on in the world around her, but still here for us to admire and wonder at.

Some 19th-century sampler verses

On Virtue
> Know now that truth, enough for men to know,
> Virtue alone is Happiness below
> The only point where human bliss stands still
> And tastes the good, without the fall to ill,
> Where only merit constant pay receives,
> Is blest in what it takes and what it gives.
>
> Elizabeth Goldspink 1811

> While beauty like a tulip gay
> In form and hue declines
> Virtue has charms that ne'er decay
> And lovely still it shines.
> This Ornament may I prefer—
> Though Others it despise—
> Nor let the Proud my mind deter
> Should all against me rise
>
> Jean Ruddle 1821

36

Chapter 5

WELSH SAMPLERS
EARLY AMERICAN SAMPLERS

Welsh Samplers

It is extremely interesting to see how samplers vary in different parts of the British Isles. A close study of each area brings out this fact very clearly. One might expect to find a difference in those of Ireland—which is a separate island—but Welsh and Scottish samplers each have their own style. The Welsh country has a beauty entirely of its own and her children have always had the ability to express it, not only in their music and poetry, but in their ancient carvings on wood and stone, and especially in their folk art.

'Treen' collectors have come to recognize the symbols which are always a feature of Welsh love-tokens the village lads carved on the spoons or knitting sheaths made for their sweethearts: a 'heart', meaning 'I love you'; a 'wheel', meaning 'I will work for you'; and another design rather like an elongated four-leaf clover which stands for something deeper—the 'soul'—'I will pray for you'.

That these symbols should be reflected in their needlework is not surprising. What *is* surprising is that 'reading' Welsh samplers is as fascinating as reading a fairy tale: one never knows what motif or object will be portrayed. One thing seems certain: the child must have designed some part of the sampler herself, and simply put into stitchery what she might have drawn on paper. This is evident in the samplers of both Mary Lewis and Margaret Morgan (see Plates 12 and 13). The former has put many traditional motifs into her sampler (worked in 1824). These were probably copied from earlier samplers, but only a child would place such very large squirrels on

37

12. Multi-motif Sampler. Coloured silks on tammy. Worked by Mary Lewis, 182·
(National Museum of Wale

'Ravens feeding Elijah' (top). 'Flight into Egypt' (bottom). Silk on tammy.
ked by Margaret Morgan, Westbrook School, 1839. (*National Museum of Wales*)

such very small trees. And she has had a free hand in the seascape pictured below. She must have lived near a harbour, for there are five ships sailing on a calm sea, yet one is sinking (a submerged rock?) and the central ship is surely a child's idea of one of the new steamships, with smoke coming out of a central funnel? Margaret Morgan has been very biblically minded, for she has embroidered on her sampler Elisha in the wilderness being fed by two ravens. Below, Moses is being discovered in the bullrushes, with Egyptian palm trees and background pyramids, flanked by a version of the 'flight into Egypt'; while overhead, astonishingly, sails a tiny balloon, in which are two men waving flags. But one cannot giggle, for the verse reads

'There is a time when I must die,
Nor can I tell how soon 'twill come,
A thousand children young as I,
Are called by Death to hear their doom.'

The National Folk Museum of Wales has many delightful, well-catalogued samplers, some with words in the national language, but, like the early American samplers, they are at least twenty years behind the English examples. My favourite is that of Leah Samuel (see Plate 14). It includes all the necessary ingredients of a good sampler: a magnificent church at the top, a flowing stream with a bridge, and a little cottage beside it with diamond-paned windows. The flowers are beautiful, forming a three-sided border. Even the verses are in Welsh, and the English translation reads

A Hundred Years From Now

A hundred years from now some of my ancestors
Were red cheeked and in great numbers on earth
But today quietly lying in their graves.
I shall be the same a hundred years from now.

I am in a very turbulent world
Sometimes happy sometimes sad,
On occasions walking in silken dresses,
On occasion hungry and without a penny in the chest.

Leah Samuel 1840

Can Mlynedd I'llawr.

can mlynedd i nawr yr oedd rhai o fy nheidia
Yn wridgoch eu pruddiau eur-lwythau ar lawr:
Ond heddyw yn dawel yn gorwedd mewn beddau
Run modd byddaf finnau can mlynedd i nawr

Rhyw fyd cymmysgedig ywr un ag wyf ynddo
Ar brydiau rwy'n llawen ac weithiau yn drist
Weithiau mewn gwisgoedd sidanaidd yn rhodio
Ac weithiau'n newynog heb geiniog i'n y gist.

Leah Samuel.
May 1840

14. 'Church and Cottage' with Welsh words. Silks on tammy. Worked by Leah Samuel, 1840. (See text for English translation) (*National Museum of Wales*)

41

An English 18th-century sampler containing a 'picture' would be a fine example of most meticulous needlework with a flower border worked in sampler stitch in a very restrained fashion, taking great care to keep the border subordinate to the main feature. Not so the Welsh needlewoman. Her border consists of two vases of flowers containing a riot of blooms in a normal embroidery stitch, with exotic birds and butterflies taking their place among them (very like the 17th-century Dutch flower pictures where flowers of every season are pictured together in one vase). Consequently, the Welsh girl's work is lively and imaginative, and obviously she enjoyed doing it.

The *sampler as a form of needlework* was evidently very popular in Wales, and not just as an exercise to be done at school, for it continued (minus the alphabet and numerals) almost to the end of the 19th century.

Early American Samplers

In the 18th century, English colonists arriving in America took all their household goods with them, and these would naturally have included samplers among the sewing tools and materials. These, and samplers made subsequently until America became independent, may, therefore, for the purpose of this book, be considered British. Indeed, I am very glad this *is* so, because they are of great importance to the historical appreciators of such work.

An American friend, Mr. Theodore H. Kapnek, has a wonderful collection of American samplers, and I owe my thanks to him for being able to describe some of them which have recently been on exhibition at the Museum of American Folk Art in New York.

The one illustrated in Plate 15 was worked by Sarah Silsbe, of Boston, Massachusetts, in 1748. The inscription reads: 'Sarah Silsbe is my name. I belong to the British Nation. Boston is my dwelling place and Christ my salvation. When I am dead and in my grave and all my bones are rotten, When this you see, remember me and never let me be forgotten'. Sarah was ten years old when she did this work, and as long as reproductions of it are published, she certainly will not be forgotten. The

15.   Early American Sampler. Worked by Sarah Silsbe, aged 10, of Boston, Massachusetts, in 1748. A deliciously naive portrayal of Adam and Eve, and a leering serpent.

picture on this sampler is a deliciously naive one of Adam and Eve, each waving an apple about, which they have obviously been tempted to take by a leering serpent wound round the tree.

One of the greatest differences between American and English samplers is that far more of those made in America seem to have been worked at school rather than home. In many cases the girl embroidered the name and place of the school on her sampler, and the history of these schools is readily available in America. In Britain far more girls were educated at home and taught needlework by their mother or governess, and it is rare to see either the name of a place or a school on the samplers they made. When they *do* occur, it is nearly always on the embroidered maps, which were 'set tasks' for girls leaving boarding schools. Early American samplers were embroidered with silk on linen (other materials were introduced later). The dyes used for colouring these silks came mostly from indigenous plants, varying according to locality. The size of the early samplers was eight or nine inches wide, and as long as was necessary to contain the work. This shape seems to have continued until about 1760 or so, when square or oblong ones became popular. At this time the early forms of 'bars' of different kinds of stitches were dropped in favour of more interesting subjects. The ideas for these were probably taken from old family samplers still to be found tucked away in drawers or work-baskets; subjects such as Adam and Eve, the house with members of the family in the fields or garden outside, familiar animals and flowers such as roses, tulips and honeysuckle, as well as the ubiquitous strawberry. But crowns, lions and unicorns, and the interminable rows of family initials were dropped. The American sampler finally emerged as a lovely unstilted, lively creation, with one difference from the British variety: it began to emerge as a *needlework picture*, in which part of the canvas was often filled in with some form of stitching, and round which borders of naturalistic, *not* stylized, flowers were embroidered. But the old idea of calling this work a sampler, to be signed and dated, still obtained, and was continued for about twenty or thirty years after it had ceased to be done in England.

Texts occur on the early samplers and, later on, verses were included which bore a great resemblance to those found on

English samplers of an earlier date. After America became independent, the character of the verses changed and displayed a morbid preoccupation with early death; quite unsuited to the content of the sampler itself. Take, for instance, these examples:

'The rising morning can't assure
That we shall end the day.
For death stands ready at the door
To take our lives away.'

'And must this body die
The mortal frame decay,
And must those active limbs of mine
Lie mouldering in the clay.'

'Only waiting till the Angels open wide the mystic gate
At whose feet I long have lingered, weary, poor and desolate.
Even now I hear their footsteps, and their voices far away
If they call me I am waiting, only waiting to obey.'

'Death like an overflowing stream,
Sweeps us away—our life's a dream
An empty tale, a morning flower,
Cut down and withered in an hour.'

After such verses as these, one reads with pleasure the short verse, common to samplers on both sides of the Atlantic:

'This I did to let you see
What care my parents took of me.'

After all these pious sentiments had been dutifully embroidered with so much care, one hopes the children ran out to play into the fields or gardens so realistically displayed elsewhere on their canvases.

16. 'House with peacocks and deer'. Coloured silks on linen.
Unnamed but dated 1828.

Chapter 6

SCOTTISH SAMPLERS
IRISH SAMPLERS

Scottish Samplers

One of the most interesting Scottish samplers I have seen was worked by Susan Kinnear of Dundee, in 1807 (see Plate 17). It is a 'tour de force', for no canvas of this size could be covered more closely with interesting motifs.

The ground is of tammy, and the embroidery is done in very brightly coloured silks. A row of family initials runs across the top. Her father's and mother's initials follow next, in very large, elaborate letters. There are the usual trees, and the flowers include tulips and a fleur-de-lys. There are two dogs, four birds, and two hearts, while two angels in a horizontal position are lustily blowing trumpets. The main subject is the Tree of Life, which is well supplied with apples, but no serpent. Adam and Eve stand on either side of the tree, named, so that one should have no difficulty in distinguishing them!

There is a very similar sampler of roughly the same period in the Royal Scottish Museum, Edinburgh (see Plate 18). It is full of different alphabets and fascinating motifs, including two peacocks with 'open'-eyed tails, and a border of strawberries. These are considered to be signs of Scottish origin (but are also found on samplers from other countries). At the end of the third line the child has worked 'A.F. aged 9' followed by the figures 96. The sampler is believed to have been worked by Ann Finlayson, Bilston Inn, Midlothian, in 1796.

Other Scottish samplers I have had have been much later in date (round about 1840–50). These were all much larger, being about eighteen inches to two feet wide, and square or oblong in shape. All had imposing frames of walnut, mahogany

47

17. 'Adam and Eve with the Tree of Life'. Worked with coloured silks on tammy by Susan Kinnear. Dundee, 1807. *(C. & J. Toller)*

18. 'House and Garden'. Worked in coloured silks and chenille on tammy with a strawberry border by Ann Walker at the turn of the 18th century.

(*Royal Scottish Museum*)

or rosewood. Some were of pine painted to simulate these woods. The samplers were all very similar in content, having wide embroidered borders of stylized flowers or geometric designs, and were worked on fine tammy gauze grounds. The favourite motifs were large buildings: castles, Georgian mansions complete with stabling and dovecotes; pele towers, churches, and a great favourite—Solomon's temple. The alternatives to buildings were shepherds and shepherdesses with flocks of sheep; stags and dogs of all sizes, and birds of all kinds.

One very large, magnificent sampler was worked by a young married woman and contained all the names of both sides of her husband's large family. At the bottom, very beautifully worked, was the family residence, a most imposing building.

All these large, late samplers had one thing in common: the muted colours of the silk and wool embroidery threads, consisting of olive greens, jaded reds and blues, ambers, rusts and old golds. I find this hard to account for, as I am sure it was possible to get much brighter colours at this time, judging by needlework pictures of the same period. Were some Scottish ladies still dependent on home-made dyes? Or did they genuinely prefer sombre shades? Late samplers of this kind were being done elsewhere in Britain in much brighter colours. These Scottish ones, perhaps, were all products of one locality or school.

Some Scottish samplers bear the name of the school as well as that of the child. Two such were Lady Amelia Murray's School at Forester's Croft, Perthshire, and that of Lady Rosebery's School at Cramond. Both these schools were started in order to educate the daughters of the estate workers.

Irish Samplers

Southern Ireland (17th and 18th century)
Irish embroidery, like that of other Celtic countries, inherited an unusual flowing type of design, which owed a great deal to that found on their national stone and wood carvings. It should be remembered also that, being a Catholic country, much of their ecclesiastical needlework was still intact on the hangings and vestments of cathedrals and religious houses. Pieces had

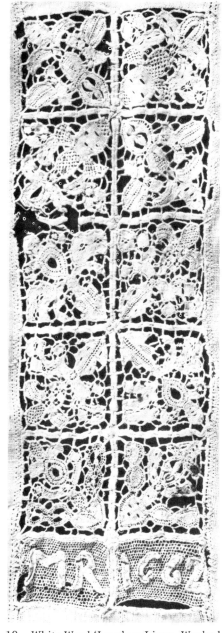

19.   White Wool 'Lace' on Linen. Worked
by a lady, M.R., in Co. Wexford, 1662.
(National Museum Dublin)

from time to time to be replaced, especially such things as white linen altar cloths and vestments, which would become weakened through use and constant washing. Consequently, there was a great need to teach embroidery, probably in the form of samplers.

The Irish have always been noted for their fine embroidery on white linen, so that learning the art of cut- and drawn-work was essential, and their samplers from the 17th century onwards bear witness to this (see Plate 19).

Incidentally, the celebrated Mary Delany, who lived in Dublin from 1746-1767, during the time her husband was Dean of Down, was greatly struck with the beauty of this embroidery, and according to one of her letters home, wore a head-dress of it when paying a duty visit to the Court of St. James.

The designs of the late 17th and 18th centuries were probably influenced by those introduced by English girls who had come to live in this part of the country in and around Dublin, which was under English rule. Sadly, much needlework and fine embroidery must have been destroyed since then, during the various troubles which have beset this beautiful country. However, many examples of work can be seen at the National Museum of Ireland in Dublin.

Northern Ireland

When I wrote to the Museum at Belfast about Northern Irish samplers, I was informed that their collection had perished in a fire, and they suggested I should get in touch with the Ulster Folk and Transport Museum at Cultra in Co. Down. This I did, and received a list of available photographs and much valuable information on their collection of samplers from Northern Ireland.

These samplers, in fact, are not unlike the English with respect to age, arrangement of subjects, and general content. The earliest (see Plate 20), worked by Mary Clay in 1716, is extremely interesting historically. Unfortunately, we do not know in what part of Northern Ireland she lived, but she was evidently being brought up to be a loyal British subject, for the most important part of her sampler consists of a prayer,

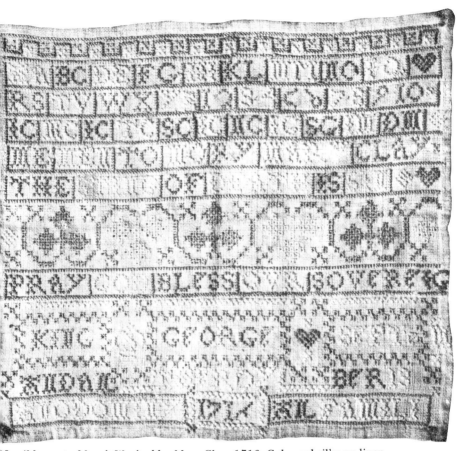

20. 'Memento Mory'. Worked by Mary Clay, 1716. Coloured silks on linen.
(*Ulster Folk and Transport Museum*)

not only for the King, but for 'all the Royal Family'. There is a curious arrangement of the sampler's date of completion, which is therefore rather hard to decipher. Here is a translation:

'May God bless our Sovereign King George [I] and all the Royal Family.

September 18 Anno dominy 1716'

It is a small sampler, worked on linen in blue, white, and green silk.

Two other Irish samplers illustrated (see Plates 21 and 22) are dated 1736 and 1770, respectively. They are in the traditional narrow width of the 17th century, and the work on both of them is reminiscent of this earlier needlework. For instance, neither of them include the letter 'J' in the alphabet, and by 1770 one might have expected some sort of picture to appear. The needlework pattern books now being published in England had not perhaps as yet reached Ireland, and one must not forget that such publications would not be cheap, and might be considered more suitable for a wealthy gentlewoman for whom embroidery was a pastime, than for children who could quite well copy the samplers of their mother, or even their grandmother. I have a feeling that this is probably what happened, and Mary Kirke at the tender age of *seven* must have been copying for some time to have achieved such a satisfying piece of work (see Plate 21). She illustrates four alphabets, three sets of figures, three lines of initials, and a wonderful edge of grapes at the bottom, and that, moreover, in Holbein stitch. I would advise any readers to use a magnifying glass in order to realize fully the beauty of this child's handiwork. Many 19th-century samplers survive, mostly signed and dated, and often give the name of the place of residence as well. (I wish this practice had been more universal.)

Numerals and alphabets were as much taught to the females in the National Schools of Ireland in the middle-19th century as in those of other parts of Great Britain, the idea being that this was a most useful thing to learn, despite the fact that marking ink was now being manufactured. One great objection to the use of marking ink is that, combined with beautiful needlework on garments, or embroidered handkerchiefs, it looks out of place and ugly. A great many girls at this time

21.   Worked by Mary Kirke, aged 7, 1736. Coloured
silks on linen.   (*Ulster Folk and Transport Museum*)

earned their living as sewing maids, and they would be expected to know how to mark linen.

We regret the many beautiful samplers wantonly destroyed in Ulster, but it is consoling to know that in the Royal Scottish Museum at Edinburgh there are two Irish samplers, both of interest. The first is

'A linen sampler 16½ ins x 2 ins, embroidered in coloured woollen and silk threads, the lettering in navy thread. Three alphabets in a conventional floral border, and a verse:

> Abroad, at home; in weal or woe
> That service which to Heaven you owe
> That bounden service duly pay
> And God shall be thy strength alway
> > Elizabeth Chicester. Mrs Logan's School Larne 1832'

The second is a very pretty sampler worked on a wool ground with coloured woollen and silk threads. The edges are bound with green silk linen. It consists of alphabets, numerals and a three-verse hymn. What makes it outstanding is the border of naturalistic roses, shamrocks and thistles. The inscription reads:

'Martha Taylor. Belfast. November 1836.'

22. Worked by Sarah Robinson, 1770.
Coloured silks on linen.
            (*Ulster Folk and Transport Museum*)

Chapter 7

SOME HINTS ON THE CARE OF SAMPLERS

IT IS MOST IMPORTANT to remove samplers from ill-fitting frames, or from those where the backing paper has perished. Dust is one of the greatest enemies of samplers, and the amount of dust that can filter through the smallest of cracks is astonishing. Nowadays, with central heating and vacuum cleaners, there is not so much dust as there was fifty years or more ago when samplers became fashionable.

I have extracted quite a lot of dust—coal dust chiefly—from even well-framed samplers, where the backing wood had cracked down the middle and shrunk away from the sides of the frames, thereby giving space for dust to enter—which it did—with horrible consequences to the samplers. Wooden backings constitute another danger, for wood grows dark with age, and as it darkens it discolours the sampler, and there is no way of getting rid of this discolouration that does not affect the sampler; one cannot bleach the linen on which it was worked without fading the embroidery silks.

Remove all old wood backing, and the rusty nails and brads that hold it in place, then very gently remove the sampler. There may be another snag here: 18th-century samplers were tacked round the *rim* of a wooden framework. When this has been done there is no cause for anxiety, but during reframing at a later period they were *cut away* from this stretcher (it was too difficult to remove the often-rusty tacks). The sampler was then *glued* round the edges of a stout cardboard backing, and as it might need cleaning and repairing, it has somehow to be removed. This takes a lot of time and trouble, to avoid damaging an often-fragile sampler. In some cases it can be removed by inserting a fine long darning needle between the sampler and the cardboard, beginning at one of the corners and separating the two substances gently and slowly so that the sampler remains unharmed.

There is another way in which previous amateur framing may cause trouble. It occurred when, before reframing a cut-away sampler, it was *nailed* to the front of the stretcher. In order to prevent the nails from showing, a gilt inset was then placed over them inside the frame. This inset not only covered the nails, but part of the sampler too, often an important part such as a date.

There is only one thing to be done here: remove the tacks with the greatest care, then draw the displaced threads together as much as possible over the holes the tacks had made, and press under a slightly dampened cloth. If a hole should need darning, a matching thread should be used. This is really a job for an expert darner to do.

To remove the dust is now the next operation. Shake the sampler gently and blow away any clinging dust. If it proves obstinate, place the sampler under a piece of net, anchor each corner with a pin and then go over it slowly and gently with a hand vacuum cleaner. This will draw the dust through the net without the cleaner coming into actual contact with the sampler.

Though this process will remove all loose dust, it will not remove any dirty marks left by the dust. These can probably be removed by gentle rubbing with soft white breadcrumbs. A little of this treatment should be tried first on the back of the sampler. Gentle rubbing will not hurt the linen or tammy background, but the embroidery silk is very fragile, and one might rub it away as well as the dust. It is terrifying to see the lettering completely disappear! Cotton, linen and woollen threads are much more hardy. If it is safe to continue the process, then turn the sampler over on to a stout piece of clean white paper and rub gently all over, changing the breadcrumbs as soon as they become dirty. New bread rolls are the easiest thing to use. Cut one in half and pull away the crust for an inch or two (crust should never come into contact with the embroidery in case it pulls a thread). Dark stains due to wood backing are practically irradicable.

Despite a popular idea that samplers can be washed, this should never be done. A tammy background will shrink, being of wool, and certainly the colours will fade, as they were made at home of vegetable dyes, which are not fast. They will certainly run all over the backing; green and black are the worst in this respect. *More samplers have been ruined by being washed than by any other cause.* Anything too fragile to be cleaned with breadcrumbs should be placed between two pieces of clean white paper or rolled up in a clean white cloth and put away for several days. It is surprising how much cleaner it will appear after a week or so of this treatment, which can be repeated, using fresh paper or cloth.

Mending

This should only be taken in hand by an expert needlewoman, for it is not an easy job. Even an expert sometimes has difficulty in finding antique linen, silks, and so on, with which to do the work. Modern colours and man-made fibres will not match either in colour or constitution, and will therefore not merge properly with the original. It is a good idea to collect fragments of antique material from which threads can be drawn for darning backgrounds; or silk and wool threads can be carefully unpicked for mending the actual embroidery. White thread can be dyed to the requisite shade for mending unbleached or brownish linen by dipping in cold tea of varying strengths (our ancestresses used the water in which rusty nails had been soaking to obtain this shade!).

All 17th-century and 18th-century samplers should *always* be left for experts to deal with.

Framing

Frames on old samplers are often the original ones, or good early-20th century copies of black and gilt 'Hogarth' frames. In these cases the frames can be used over again, after being meticulously cleaned, taking special care with the glass, which should be crystal clear. Any backing wood should be thrown away and stout millboard substituted. Apart from the question of discolouration, thin board is a happy hunting ground for wood-worms, which bore right through the wood and make holes in the sampler. It is also liable to shrinkage and cracking, causing gaps through which dust and moths will surely enter in the course of time.

The glass should be fixed to the inside of the frame with narrow strips of gummed paper, *not* 'Sellotape'. Care should be taken that the paper is not visible through the glass. 17th and early 18th-century samplers should be framed between two pieces of glass. This not only reveals the wonderful neatness of the back of this early work, but shows the colours of the embroidery silks in their original unfaded condition.

If the words are difficult to read on a sampler, through fading, it should be held up to the light, when it becomes quite readable. Framing *between* glass is a great advantage here, as there is no difficulty with a solid back. A sampler framed in glass is free from every harmful agent except *strong light*. A warning would not come amiss here: *never* hang samplers, or needlework of any description, in a strong light, either natural or artificial; it not only fades the colours, but can rot the silk or satin on which the embroidery is worked.

Original frames often seem to be a very dark, heavy black, quite unsuitable for the samplers. In nearly every case, on close inspection it will be found that cheap black paint (easily removable) has been superimposed on to a gilt frame. Why anyone should paint gilt frames black is a mystery. One romantic (but maybe quite true) theory is that, after the death of Nelson (which upset the English people more than is generally realized), all frames were painted black as a mark of respect, and deep mourning for a nation's loss.

Any really good samplers should be placed in a new frame by a professional, and care should be taken in choosing the right kind of frame, which should enhance the sampler and not bury it. Bird's-eye maple, a popular choice, should only be used for *late* samplers worked round about 1840, as this wood did not become fashionable until then. Narrow gilt or walnut frames are, in my opinion, the most suitable.

If the sampler to be framed is embroidered right up to the edge, neatly seam a piece of antique tape all round it. The *edge* of the frame will cover this and the whole of the sampler will then be displayed. Very often the edges of a beautiful sampler are partially obliterated by the frame, even covering beginnings of words, which makes it more difficult to read them.

INDEX